Home, Hearth, and Oreos

By J. Suthern Hicks

A One Act Comedy-Drama

Cover Design: J. Suthern Hicks
A Shophar So Good Book: www.shopharsogood.com

ISBN: 0997077824
ISBN-13: 978-0997077827

PRODUCTION OVERVIEW

Cast Size
1m, 2f

Duration
60 minutes (1 hour)

Subgenre
Southern, Comedy-Drama, Older Female Lead, Character-Driven

Target Audience
Appropriate for all audiences

Additional Information
A grandmother wants nothing more than to see her grandchildren for the first time. But time is no longer her friend. By employing a little humor, some manipulation, and her nurse, Mary, she sets out to meet her grandchildren. But she soon finds out that her son, Mike, may not be able to meet her expectations.   A gem of a play about family, love, psychology, and longing. The honesty of this play and the manner in which the characters have been brought to life will move audience and participants in a most profound way.

CONSIDERATIONS

Performing Groups
High School, College Theatre, Community Theatre, Dinner Theatre, Professional Theatre, Shoestring Budget, Blackbox, Second Stage, Church/Religious Groups

LICENSE DETAILS

Minimum Fee: $30 per performance
Contact: HumbleEntertainment@yahoo.com

PRODUCTION DETAILS

Time Period: Before Cell Phones
Duration: 60 minutes (1 hour)
Setting: Simple bedroom in a convalescent center
Additional Features: No intermission
Features: No special costumes or set pieces

For
PEGGY COZZI

,

The first performance of Home, Hearth, and Oreos was given at the Taber Theatre, Los Angeles, on May 21, 1994, by the Toluca Lake Players. It was Directed by J. Suthern Hicks and produced by Jean Sportelli. The cast was as follows:

Mom	Peggy Cozzi
Mike	Brian Fairlee
Mary	Joyce English

CAST

In Order of Appearance

MOM
MIKE: HER SON
MARY: A NURSE

CONTENTS

The action takes place in MOM'S
room in a convalescent home.

TIME: Before Cell Phones

SCENE I
A Fall Evening.

SCENE II
A Week Later.

SCENE III
A Few Days Later.

SCENE I

Mom's bedroom in a convalescent center in a small southern town.

A fall evening.

The curtain opens to reveal a small room. A bed, dresser, two chairs, and a small window are the most outstanding features. Colors are warm and bright—representing the time of an older lady's youth. There are not too many wall hangings or knickknacks as this is thought to be a temporary place of residence by the occupant. One 8"X10" photograph and a photo album are placed prominently on the dresser. It's a time before cell phones, iPads, and other electronic distractions. Mike is sitting in the chair next to the window thumbing through a magazine. He is tall and looks younger than his middle-aged status. He is of average looks and carries himself confidently. He talks without an accent and as if someone important might be recording his every word. Mom is across the room whittling in her favorite chair. She is humming. She has a complete head of grey hair and many wrinkles. She is old but still moves quite freely, except when seeking sympathy or attention. She speaks with a soft southern accent—consisting mainly of shortened words. Her bright flowery sun dress reveals her round figure.

Presently, Mike abruptly sets down a magazine.

MIKE: Mom, I wish you would refrain from humming while I'm trying to read.

MOM: Well, it's just as quiet as a mouse peein' on cotton in here and I can't stand it! You would think that a person with all your intellectual depth could concentrate. You come by your lack of discipline quite honestly. (*Short pause.*) I don't know how many times your father had to eat his three-minute eggs two minutes overdone. He could sure tell the difference too. I never seen anything like it in all my life... (*after a pause.*) It's no wonder he died of a heart attack at such a young age. Of course, we didn't think nothin' about cholesterol back then. I don't do a whole lot of thinking about it now. Your Aunt Desi used to say he died of heart failure from arguing about those cotton pickin' eggs bein' over-done. I told him to get me a timer if he wanted three-minute eggs cooked three minutes. I got better things to do with my time than sit around lookin' at a couple of eggs boilin'. That's exactly what I used to tell him. (*Beat.*) I guess twenty years of that could put any man in the grave.

MIKE: (*walks to dresser and picks up an 8"X10" picture*). Would you like to go out for a walk or something?

The courtyard is quite picturesque this time of year–golds and warm yellows hanging from the trees. (*After no response.*) When did I give you this photo of the kids?

MOM: Right after you stuck me in this darlin' little home for the elderly. "It's either her or me." That's what she said. That's what your blushin' bride revealed at the dinner table in front of God and everyone. I would have shoved those peas up her nose had I known she could talk with a napkin wrapped around her throat. I don't care too much for her. Did you know that, Mike?

MIKE: I'm so good at opening those doors, aren't I mother?

MOM: Well, you do (*Mike mouths in unison.*) come by it honestly. (*Mom resumes whittling and humming.*)

MIKE: What is that anyway?

MOM: It's going to be a night stick for Mrs. Rippy in room 304. Or is she in 403? She's scared to death a big black man is gonna take her head off during one of her naps. I think she is prejudice, bless her heart. She grew up in the South. Not that that has a thing to do with bein' prejudice. Cause Lord knows I am not prejudice and a body can't get no further south than Louisiana. (*After a pause.*) Those male nurses love to tease Mrs. Rippy. I told her I'd make this night stick so she could whop 'em on the head. She won't use it unless it's pretty lookin', so I'm carvin' roses in the handle.

MIKE: I meant what is that tune you were humming?

MOM: Oh, just a little ditty I made up.

MIKE: You used to hum that when I was a child. Whenever I had a bad dream or if the weather was stormy, you came into my room and sang me to sleep.

MOM: Yes, I guess I did. Come to think of it, I used to sing that same tune to your sister. But she didn't take to it quite like you did. You were such a sweet little boy. (*Under her breath but obviously wanting to be heard.*) It's amazing what forty-five years can do to a person!

MIKE: (*casually*). What was that, Mom?

MOM: Nothing dear, nothing at all.

MIKE: (*impatiently, looking out window*). I wish that tow truck would get a move on. Maybe I should call Kate and tell her I'll be a little late getting home.

MOM: That might be a good idea. Those service people have a way with showin' up too late or too early. Did I ever tell you about the time the roach man came knockin' on my door at five in the mornin'? It was just after your dad died. Well, Lord, I thought I was gonna palpitate! I was so scared my body was shakin' like a washin' machine on spin cycle with one towel short of a balanced load. I didn't know if I should call the police or run out the back door.

4

MIKE: (*after short pause*). Well? (*She says nothing.*) What did you do?

MOM: About what?

MIKE: Did you run or call the police?

MOM: I couldn't run out the back door. What would the neighbors think about me streakin' around in my petticoat? I could just hear 'em talkin' about me the next day, "Did you see that fat lady next door runnin' around the street stark naked. Just as naked as a wet pig she was!" Yup, that's what they would of said. And the police were out of the question because the mice had eaten plumb through the telephone wire. Or who knows, it may have been those Spanish roaches. Have you ever seen a Spanish roach? They are gigantic!

MIKE: (*after a short pause*). Mom?

MOM: Yes, Son?

MIKE: So, what did you do about the exterminator?

MOM: Well I answered the door. What else was I going to do?

MIKE: Never-mind. I think I will just go out to the front desk and call Kate. She probably has the kids waiting up on me. (*Mike proceeds to open the door.*)

MOM: Alright, Son. You be sure and tell Kate I said to come visit me one of these days...and to bring those grandkids of mine with her, of course.

MIKE: Let's not get into this every time I come to visit.

(*Sympathetically.*) Just this once, okay? I won't be long. (*Mike exits.*)

MOM: (*humming quietly as she gets up and peeks out door. She energetically tip toes to dresser and picks up picture of grandkids. She places the picture where Mike was sitting earlier. She stands back as if viewing a work of art.*) What beautiful children.

MIKE: (*enters just as Mom sits back down*). Just as I thought. She had the kids waiting up on me. It's a good thing I called.

MOM: (*smiling*). You just have a seat and I'll see if I can't keep you entertained until that tow service shows up...Did I finish tellin' you about the roach man?

MIKE: I think so mom. You don't need to entertain me. I simply enjoy being with you.

MOM: That's nice to hear, dear. (*She begins humming.*)

MIKE: (*after an awkward silence*). So tell me, Mom, what's new in your life? Are you ever going to get a new roommate?

MOM: You broke your previous record—that's new.

MIKE: (*with some hesitation*). I don't understand.

MOM: You have been here forty-five minutes. Of course, I'm includin' the time you left to make the phone call to the towin' service and...well...I forgot to time your call to Kate. But nevertheless, you have been in the building under which I am housed for a total of forty-five minutes. (*She immediately begins to whittle at*

6

an awkwardly fast pace.)

MIKE: (*sternly*). Do you insist, (*Pauses to gain his composure.*) on starting an argument every time I come here? Just once I thought I could leave here without an argument chasing me out the door. If it's not about not getting to see the kids, it's about my visits with you. Can't we just sit here quietly until the tow truck comes?

MOM: (*after another awkward pause*). The weather sure was nice today.

MIKE: Yes, it was. (*Mom begins to hum. Every time Mike turns a page in his magazine she hums louder.*) Mom, you know I've tried to get Kate to bring the kids over, but she just feels it's not the proper thing to do.

MOM: Proper? What has proper got to do with it? A grandmother gettin' to see her own son's children?

MIKE: Oh, you know Kate and her silly ideas.

MOM: No, actually I don't.

MIKE: Maybe I can bring the kids on my next visit.

MOM: You've said that before.

MIKE: I know, Mom...It's just going to take a little time.

MOM: (*changing the subject*). Do you remember when we used to take trips on the lake? You would read stories to me while I would row around. You were such a tiny little boy.

MIKE: The Adventures of Huckleberry Fin. God how I loved

that story. Still do.

MOM: You were such an excellent reader. Always actin' out the characters. I was scared half to death you might want to be an actor when you grew up.

MIKE: What about when I got big enough to row the boat? You weren't such a bad reader yourself. (*Laughs*.) Of course, Webster wasn't exactly on my list of literary greats. You always hoped I would learn a new word for the day...(*Smiling*.) I always did.

MOM: Tell me! The very next day you would use it over and over and over and over. I thought you were goin' to drive your dad plumb out of his mind.

MIKE: I never knew you even noticed.

MOM: Notice? I wrote down every word you learned. It was somewhat of a game to me. I never knew what the word was goin' to be until the next day. They never failed to surprise me.

MIKE: What surprised you?

MOM: The words you chose to remember.

MIKE: I sure wish they would have surprised father.

MOM: You tried relentlessly to get his attention with those over ripe words. I don't think any of us could get his attention too easily. He used to work so hard. That seemed to be all he ever thought about.

MIKE: You noticed that too? I wondered.

MOM: I noticed lots of things. But back in my day it wasn't the woman's place to question the ways of her man.

He tried his best to be everything he could to us. And I suppose he did a pretty good job.

MIKE: Are you kidding? That man was stuck in a world all his own.

MOM: I guess you have a right to question your father's actions, now that you have children of your own. Uh, you do have children, don't you? I can't ever be too sure. Bein' that I've never seen them in real life or anything. Well, I reckon only time will tell if history repeats itself.

MIKE: What do you mean by that?

MOM: I wouldn't judge your father till you've walked around in his shoes for a good spell.

MIKE: Don't worry. I do not plan on raising my kids to think that I hate them. Everything I do is for them. Every time I punch the time card, I'm thinking about nothing but my kids. I've been working sixty plus hours a week to save money for their college tuition, and things like braces for Hannah. Everything I do is for them.

MOM: Do they know that?

MIKE: Well, of course they know it.   Sometimes I think you just try to antagonize me, mother.

MOM: Oh, and I suppose that's why you got me that crazy book called Antagony for my birthday last year.

MIKE: It's Antigony, Mother. Let me put it this way. When James Paul is ready to go to med-school, he won't

have to worry about paying one dime. I think he'll
figure out how much I love him.

MOM: I beg your pardon? You need to get with the program.
What makes you think Hannah won't want to go to
medical school?

MIKE: Hannah can go wherever she wants and study
whatever she sees fit. I'll have enough saved for both
of them.

MOM: What do you wear? A size nine?

MIKE: Shoe size? (*Mom nods yes.*) That's about right, why?

MOM: Your dad wore a size nine and a half. Your feet'll
spread a bit as you age.

MIKE: So what are you getting at?

MOM: You're not half as bright as I think you are. For
someone who dislikes his father as much as you
proclaim, you're sure doin' a heck of a job followin'
in his footsteps.

MIKE: What has my wanting to send the kids to prominent
schools got to do with my dad?

MOM: You should be findin' that out in about ten years.

MIKE: What do you mean?

MOM: I remember very clearly the day you told your father
you were not goin' to law school. I never saw a man's
heart more broken in all my life than your fathers
was on that day.

MIKE: He never gave a damn about what I did.

MOM: Watch your mouth! I suppose it's about time I told

you this. And what the heck, since you're stuck here, I may as well spill the whole sack of turnips. Your father loved you more than anything in this world. Just like you love your kids. I thought you would have figured that out by now.

MIKE: No, I don't have the same recollections as you, I guess. My memories are based on a different set of observations—like the missed football games, fishing trips, and the other things Dad was so good at avoiding.

MOM: Aw, shucks. You weren't no good at football anyway. You never could get that ball to go between those two polls. (*Laughs.*) I'm just kiddin' ya.

MIKE: I wasn't a kicker, Mom. I bet Dad didn't know what position I played either.

MOM: Your father worked a lot of long and hard hours. He saved five percent of his earnings so he could send you to the place he wished he could have gone—to school. That's the reason he never spent much time with you kids. But I can guarantee you this, he was doin' a whole lot of thinkin' about you. He loved you more than huntin' trips with his friends, more than days off from work, more than his own life. Of course there was a price to be paid. By the time you were grown he didn't really know how to relate to you. He sure wanted to though. He sure wanted to.

MIKE: Five percent?

MOM: He didn't want you to know. He didn't even tell me he had saved the money until after his heart attack.

MIKE: Why not?

MOM: His father pushed him to take over the family business. From a very young age your father knew what his father expected of him. No dreams. No hope to become his own person. Everything a young man was supposed to feel was pulled right out of him until he couldn't bear it any longer. When he left home, he never turned back...he never spoke to his father again either.

MIKE: Didn't he love him?

MOM: I suppose perhaps he did, but he never spoke much about his personal feelings, just the facts—as he remembered them. Your father never wanted that to happen between the two of you.

MIKE: I guess it backfired then, didn't it?

MOM: Oh, no. Not to him it didn't. You never left home in a mad rush. Your father got to see you turn into a man. He was always proud of you—never said so, but I could tell. He loved you so much.

MIKE: It's still hard for me to understand why he was so distant when I was a kid. I could never relate to him. I'm a father and I refuse to make the same choices he did.

MOM: The only things he did were out of love. Love for me and you kids. A rose don't make pollen for the honey bee to steal it away. A rose makes pollen for all the other little roses. Your father was a perfect rose. He might not have had the prettiest bloom, but he sure had plenty of pollen.

MIKE: I'm not sure I totally get that picture you just painted, but I appreciate the attempt. I just find it hard to forgive someone I barely knew. You must know that I loved him. As much as I might have said otherwise, I really wanted to be just like him, that's why I didn't want to go to law school. I wanted to make my way in the world like Dad did. I wanted to prove myself to him. Maybe then he would have noticed me. That's what I thought, anyway.

MOM: He noticed you.   He noticed you.
(*Mike walks over to window and stares out.*)

MOM: You see that picture over there filled up with them little ones?

MIKE: How could I miss it? You practically plaster it to my face every time I visit you.

MOM: Oh, so you noticed my cleverness? (*Smiles.*)

MIKE: Right, Mom!

MOM: Someday your kids will grow up with some of the same feelings you have about your father.   I would hate to see them use you as an example of how to deal with those feelings.

MIKE: I really doubt...

MOM: (gets dizzy, *stumbles to the floor*). Dear! I guess all

this talk of your father has got my mind overworked...
Lord knows your father could sure work me up while
he was alive. (*Laughs.*)

MIKE: (*helping her up*). Mom? Are you going to be alright?

MOM: God I hope so. There's a man down the hall that
wants to take me to dinner tomorrow.   The cook
promised us some fried food. Who knows, I may do a
little cookin' myself. (*Laughs.*)

MIKE: Here, sit down and catch your breath.

MOM: Whew! (*Fanning herself.*) I wish those yellow dots
would quit circlin' the room.

MIKE: (*bringing her a glass of water from a pitcher on the
night stand*). Here's some water...Maybe I should go
get the nurse.

MOM: Oh, no! Don't be such a ninny. I'll be just fine. (*Sips
water.*) There! Now that hit the spot. (*Fanning
herself.*) Lord bless my soul! You would think that I
was on my death bed or somethin'. I have been
havin' these spells for a month now.

MIKE: Have you seen a doctor?

MOM: Oh, yes, of course. The last one was a real doozy. If
Mary, Mary is a nurse. Have you ever met Mary?
She's just a wonder. I'm sure you would just love
Mary. I do. But don't you dare tell her I said that. She
is sassy enough without help from me... (*She stares
into space.*)

MIKE: Mom?

MOM: Oh, excuse me. Anyway, Mary caught me while I was havin' one of these spells. She kept me from splittin' my head wide open. (*Sips water.*) You know, that's what happen to Miss. Sheppard in room 801 or was it 901? No, I think it was 108. Split her head wide open... (*Pointing towards bathroom.*) Right there on her own bathroom sink! Whew! I think I need to catch my breath.

MIKE: (*heading towards door*). Are you sure I shouldn't get the nurse?

MOM: No. No. No...I'll be just fine.

MIKE: Do you need anything?

MOM: No, I'll be alright. Let me sit here and rest a moment. (*Sips more water.*) You could bring me that photo-album there on the dresser.

MIKE: (*handing her the album*). What did the doctor say?

MOM: You know how those doctors are. They don't say too much of anything. He told me to get some extra sleep and that I would be just fine. Fine for an old lady. That's what he meant. Fine since I'm near dyin' age anyway. You know they're always lookin' for extra beds in this place. Another corner to stick some old person into. One goes out on a table and another one comes rollin' in on a chair. They think I'm gonna croak like a bullfrog. They're probably takin' bets up in the lounge right now. I saw one of those pyramid games bein' passed around last week. My name was at the top! Takin' bets. That's what they're doin'!

MIKE: Mom, don't talk like that. You are not going to die.

MOM: And who are you, Doctor Marcus Welby?

MIKE: If you think you are going to be alright for the next few minutes, I'm going to go make a phone call. You look just fine to me, and your lungs certainly haven't been affected.

MOM: Don't be in such a rush. I thought we would sit here and look through the photo-album together.

MIKE: I have seen that thing a hundred times and so have you.

MOM: I only look at it so I can see my grandkids. I reckon since I've never seen 'em in real life, I should look at 'em in here just before I die to make up for the difference...as if it would.

MIKE: I wish you wouldn't talk like that. You are not going to die. I remember Grandmother would act the same silly way. From sixty on she never let a day pass without letting everyone know she was going to start digging a hole in the backyard. She just knew that her death was moments away.

MOM: And what happened? She died!

MIKE: Mom, she was one-hundred and three years old. Don't worry, you have superior genes. You are going to live many more wonderful years.

MOM: Wonderful years? Ha! Wait till your kids throw your frail ol' body into a nursin' home. (*Mumbling.*) You better bet I'll be back to see that day.

MIKE: (*sternly*). That's enough mother. I refuse to listen to those snide mumblings anymore. I have told you many times that I don't like this set up any more than you do. (*Pauses, looks out window.*) Do you think that I leave here every week with a smile on my face? Well, I don't, Mother. There have been countless hours that I sat out in that car of mine looking up at this tiny window...tears streaming down my face...trying to figure a way to get you out of this God forsaken excuse for a home. But I can't mother. God forgive me, I can't. (*Pauses.*) Every night I lie awake thinking about those boat trips you used to take me on. One hour passes, then two. I'm lucky if I fall asleep before the alarm goes off. It just gets worse and worse. (*Moves within hands reach of Mom.*) That's why I haven't been to see you much lately...the more I do, the more it hurts.

MOM: (*running her hands through his hair*). Son, I don't mean to be a burden. Lord knows you are the most important thing in my life...I couldn't love you any more than I do.

MIKE: I know you do, Mom. I know. I love you too.

MOM: I guess things just have a way of (*Not able to find the right words.*) Oh, I don't know.

MIKE: I know what you mean. (*He walks towards the picture and stares, takes a deep breath.*) So, what would you like to know about the kids?

MOM: You mean you don't mind?

MIKE: I never have...I guess I was just afraid of upsetting you too much by talking about them.

MOM: Upset me? Nonsense.

MIKE: Mom, you really are special.

MOM: It's about time you noticed! You're just like your father. It took him a decade to notice my hair had turned grey.

MIKE: Didn't you have bright red hair when you were young? (*Picks up photo-album and excitedly flips through it.*)

MOM: Memories weren't meant to last *that* long. Grey is all this ol' mind can remember. But I must confess, people did used to confuse me with Lucille Ball—that comedy actress. She was beautiful.

MIKE: Hannah's hair has erupted into the brightest fury of red you have ever laid eyes on. It's the color of hot molten rock.

MOM: Sounds like my granddaughter. Red hair has been in our family for ages.

MIKE: James Paul is at the questioning stage. Just last week he stood up in church, right in the middle of the sermon, and asked the woman sitting in front him what was wrong with her hair. Apparently, he had never seen grey hair before.

MOM: Oh, I bet that woman really got a kick out of that. Kids can sure be honest, can't they? Innocence, pure innocence.

MIKE   Yeah, they sure are.

MOM: And so inquisitive.

MIKE: James Paul is really good with his hands. He is going to make a great doctor.

MOM: Really? What school will he be attendin'?

MIKE: The best in the country, of course. I have already started his college fund. Yeah, I know what you are Thinking—just like Dad. But everything is different when you're the parent. (*She gives him a look.*) Don't look at me that way. I just want what is best for him.

MOM   What does Kate think of all this?

MIKE: She doesn't pay attention to me. She lives in a fantasy world as far as how she treats the kids. She insists on teaching Hannah at home next year. Not to give her a better education, but to keep her under lock and key. The entire Parent Teacher's Association thinks Kate's a nut. Last year she was in charge of food for an awards banquet. She served frozen dinners and then lectured everyone on how school food is trash and how would they like it if they had to eat the equivalent of a frozen dinner every day. From what I heard, people asked for seconds.

MOM: Perhaps she has the kids' best interests in mind. There is nothin' wrong with bein' protective of your children. Maybe if I had been a little more protective you wouldn't have shot your foot out in them swamp woods. The Lord knows I should have kept you from totin' that gun into them woods. But your father always wanted you to grow up manly. Manly without a foot, I guess. If it takes nearly shootin' your foot off to become a man, why can't you do it in your own backyard? That's what I asked your father.

MIKE: (*grimacing*). Please don't remind me of that wonderful experience.

MOM: (*fanning herself*). Whew! It's gettin' awful hot in here. I'm sweatin' like a yard dog. Would you be a sweetie and open that window for me? You have to push real hard. It tends to get stuck.
(*While Mike clears windowsill of clutter, Mom carefully sprawls out on floor. She then jumps up to grab a vase, smashes it on floor, and sprawls out again while howling in agony.*)

MIKE: (*turns around and shouts*). My God! Nurse! Nurse! (*Runs to door and yells out.*) Nurse! Someone get a nurse! (*He kneels next to her.*) What happened, Mom? Are you alright? (*Mary, the nurse, enters. She is black and slightly overweight. Her features are soft and warm—hiding her sometimes sarcastic personality. Although she speaks with a slight southern accent, she is educated and wise.*)

MARY: Now I ain't about to lift this woman all by myself! (*To Mike.*) Go get nurse Floyd and tell her to call the doctor.

(*He Exits.*)

MOM: (*rising off the floor*). Get your hands off me, Mary Rosalyn! Now go back and tell that doctor to stay home. (*Mom opens door and peeks out.*)

MARY: Girl, you are the strangest white woman I have ever laid eyes on! Now, is there somethin' wrong with you or are you havin' one of those out of mind experiences? (*Mary stares in bewilderment as Mom nervously keeps opening and closing the door to peek out.*) I've been readin' some books on astral projection and out of mind travel. I know how to deal with these out of mind experiences...we got a psycho ward right across the street!

MOM: Don't you threaten me, Mary Rosalyn! If you don't play along with me, I swear I'll tell weight watchers about those all-night Snicker parties in the pantry. And it's out of *body* experience.

MARY: (*moving in behind Mom*). Yeah, I wish I could get out of this body! But until I do, you had better keep that mouth shut about my eatin' habits. You hear?

MOM: (*leaning against door to keep it closed*). I hear. I've got a package of Oreos in the top right-hand drawer of my dresser if you will just play along with me. They're in a brown paper bag. (*Mom looks out door again*).

MARY: What is goin' on here?

MOM: (*impatiently*). I don't have time to explain. I'll fill you

in later. (*Mom folds down sheets on bed.*) Just do as I
do. Follow my lead. (*Mom gets into bed just before
Mike enters*).

MIKE: I told the nurse to call the doctor (*Looks at Mary.*) Is
she alright?

MARY: (*in a tone of indifference*). I think you better ask her
that.

MOM: Yes. Mary, I think you are right. I concur. It's best if I
break the news.

MIKE & MARY: (*in unison*). What news?!

MOM: Son, I only have a few weeks left to live. (*She adds a
cough. Mike falls into chair.*)

MARY: Say what? (*Mom grimaces at Mary.*) Oh, I thought
the doctor said you had a few *months* left. My bad.
(*Mary looks confused.*)

MOM: Well, Mary, that was a couple of months ago, if you
will recall.

MARY: I see. Well, listen honey, I better go see about the
arrangements. (*Mary goes to dresser and gets
Oreos.*)

MOM: (*caught off guard*). What arrangements?

MIKE: (*shocked*). Arrangements? Oh my God.

MARY: If you only have a few weeks left, we better put a rush
on that goin' away party. (*As she crosses to door.*)
Lord, how time flies. Two months gone just like that.
(*Snaps fingers.*) Well I declare, I ain't even sent out
the invitations yet. (*Mary exits.*)

MIKE: What is going on here? You were in excellent health the last time I saw you.

MOM: Yes, those were the good ol' days. What I wouldn't give to be in such good health again.

MIKE: (*incredulously*). Since last Friday?

MOM: Of course not...I just haven't been able to tell you about...about my condition. With all your problems, I didn't want to burden you any further.

MIKE: (*stunned, Mike stands next to bed*). Burden me? What were you going to do? Wait until the last minute? Or did you plan on leaving a note?

MOM: Right hand top corner drawer.

MIKE: (*walks over to dresser and retrieves note*). I don't believe this...No! I take that back. You always waited until the last minute to do everything, but this is beyond even you. (*After a pause*). I feel so ridiculous...so helpless. (*Walks to window, looks out.*) I never expected it to happen like this.

MOM: You mean knowin' ahead of time? I know how ya feel. I always figured it would have happened in my sleep...in the middle of the night. You know, during one of those dreams where you're floatin' down an endless tunnel. Only I would want my death dream to be in a tunnel with good lighting so I could see the gorgeous man next to me, naked as a jaybird...what a free fall that could turn out to be...and no guilt the next day! (*She looks at Mike, who is not amused.*)

What?

MIKE: How can you joke at a time like this?

MOM: Who's jokin'? That was a prayer, honey!

MIKE: (*slowly*). It never really hit me until right this moment. Sooner or later everyone dies. I mean everyone...dies. (*Still looking out window.*) I suppose I always depended on you to be here for me. Moms are always there when you need them, right? When Dad died, I turned to you. Whatever amount of love I had for him was instantly transferred to you. Mom, I may not have always said so, or even showed so, but I love you.

MOM: I know you do, son.

MIKE: What do we do now?

MOM: Well, I know one thing for sure. I better start workin' overtime if I want to finish Mrs. Hoaks' nightstick! Here, hand me that thing (*Pointing.*) And my whittlin' knife.

MIKE: You amaze me! How can you sit there in that bed, so calmly, and think about finishing a craft? Didn't you think that I had a right to know what was going on?

MOM: I was goin' to tell you. I just couldn't find the right time.

MIKE: Cutting it pretty damn close, don't you think?

MOM: I never did have a good sense of timing. And you had better watch that foul mouth of yours!

MIKE: A good sense of timing? In a month you may not...

MOM: Oh, shiscadoodle! You're so nervous, you look like a shakin' dog on a squirrel! Just calm down. I'll be around for a good spell yet, God willin'. Of course I haven't always been the good Christian I should...

MIKE: Mom, please stop.

MOM: Here's my strategy. I figure if I was to give this nightstick to charity, of course I'd have to call it a table leg or something—not too many people out buying rose handled nightsticks ya' know, the good Lord might just give me a few more months to finish it right nicely.

MIKE: Please stop it. I can't listen to your humor right now.

MOM: I was only tryin' to lighten the situation. You're always so serious about everything, even as a child. I never thought you'd stop cryin' when that goldfish of yours died.

MIKE: You and Dad weren't much comfort. I never forgave you two for laughing. You don't take death too seriously, do you?

MOM: It was funny! He picked a bad time to jump out of his bowl, bless his heart. That goldfish never hit the ground and as God is my witness your sister's ol' tomcat grinned from ear to ear. Never knew a cat could grin.

MIKE: I apologize for taking death too seriously. And the cat didn't grin.

MOM: All I'm sayin' is that the whole situation is in the hands of the Lord. Not the doctor and certainly not me. I don't plan on diggin' my own grave and I would appreciate it if you would wait till I'm gone before you stick your hands to a shovel. But on the other hand, it might not be a bad idea to catch one on sale...or a nice urn, maybe.

MIKE: (*looks towards door*). Every week I walk down those halls and ignore the vast amount of loneliness I see peeking out these doors and windows...I always managed to shrug it off...this place has death written all over it. (*After a pause.*) Mom, I really wish...I am really sorry for the way things turned out. If I could change anything, I would.

MOM: You have been a wonderful son. Don't let anyone tell you otherwise. You visit me once a week. Call at the right times, send flowers...There's just one thing I find hard to forgive.

MIKE: The kids, right?

MOM: They're my grandchildren! I have every right in the world to be a grandmother to those kids. And even more importantly, they deserve to know me.

MIKE: I've tried to get Kate to bring the kids down to see you, but she refuses.

MOM: I don't care what Kate thinks. You said it yourself, she's a nut.

MIKE: That was the members of the Parent Teacher's

Association, not me.

MOM: I want to know why I have been denied all these years. And don't you dare put it all on Kate's shoulders. You should have enough backbone to do what you know is right.

MIKE: Mom? I have always been honest with you, have I not?

MOM: I think so.

MIKE: Then please believe me now. I honestly don't know why Kate wants to keep the kids from seeing you. Heck, I don't even know if it's you she wants to keep them away from. I can't figure it out.

MOM: (*starting to break*). You mean you never questioned?

MIKE: Of course I did. But after a while I stopped asking why and just accepted.

MOM: (*dumbfounded*). And you just accepted?

MIKE: She is my wife and for whatever reason, as fate would have it, I love her. I know you find that hard to understand, but I do love Kate.

MOM: (*rises, sits up in bed*). I am the woman that bore you. Does that not count for just a little somethin'?

MIKE: All right! What do you want from me? What do you want me to do? I owe you everything. I realize that. (*He falls back into chair*). What do you want?

MOM: I want to see my grandchildren!

MIKE: (*flatly*). Done.

MOM: What do you mean by that?

MIKE: I mean it's done. If it causes a divorce, I don't care. You are right and I've known that all along. You have every right in the world to see your grandchildren.

MOM: (*angry*). I don't believe what I'm hearin'!

MIKE: That's what you want, isn't it?

MOM: (*reaches for her cane on the nightstand*). Do you mean to tell me that all I had to do was have it out with you? All this time has gone by all I had to do was confront you face to face? Do you know how many times I've cried because I never got to change a diaper or sing a sweet hymn to those babies—my own flesh and blood?

MIKE: You have had it out with me before mother. It's because you're ...because you're...things are just different now, okay? (*Quietly.*) I'm the bastard here. I'm the rotten son. (*Rubbing his forehead.*) I thought that things would work themselves out in time. Because that's the one thing I thought I could count on—time. Now, even the one constant of the world is laughing in my face, mocking my image of the weak husband and the rotten son. (*Mom lets out a loud moan. Mike quickly rises from chair and rushes to her side.*) What is it? Are you okay?

MOM: (*grasping Mike's arm*). Just gas.

MIKE: (*sighs, shakes his head*). What does the doctor say is wrong with you?

MOM: That isn't important.

MIKE: I would like to know. Maybe there is a specialist or something that I could find to help you.

MOM: Let's see. (*Thinking*.) I get dizzy a lot. That's on the account of my lungs fillin' up with fluid...I think that's right.

MIKE: Why are they filling up with fluid?

MOM: (*hesitates*). Why are they fillin' up with fluid? (*Flustered*.) Do you think I got a doctorate in lungs over there at the senior center? Only thing I learned there is how to fill up a bingo card. That's enough talk about this. It just makes me nervous.

MIKE: Okay, we can discuss this later, But...

(*Mary opens door and sticks her head in the room*).

MARY: The tow truck is here to take your car to the shop. (*Mary Exits*).

MIKE: (*looking at his watch*). I think I should stay a while longer until the doctor comes by...

MOM: Oh, no.   I'm tired and I need my rest. You go home and get that car of yours fixed. We wouldn't want you to miss work tomorrow. There's plenty of time to talk about all this mess.

MIKE: Are you sure?

MOM: As sure as an eagle starein' down on a rabbit.

MIKE: (*takes his mother's hand*.) Listen, Mom, I'll be back early tomorrow. I want to make sure you're okay. I also want to talk to the doctor in person.

(*Mike crosses to door as Mom stands, with cane in*

hand, to follow.)

MOM: Don't forget about your promise.
(*Standing next to Mike at door.*)

MIKE: (*kissing her forehead*). I won't. I won't ever let you down again. (*Opens door and turns back to look at Mom.*) I love you.
(*Mike exits.*)

MOM: (*quickly leans her back on the door. She then tosses her cane on the bed and walks over to dresser. She gently picks up the picture of her grandchildren and caresses it as she waltzes around the room. She hums as she dances. After a moment she pulls a tissue from her pocket and wipes a tear. Lights fade.*)

CURTAIN

END OF SCENE ONE

SCENE TWO

A week later, Mom's bedroom.

Lights rise as Mom is whittling and humming in her favorite chair. Mary has just measured Mom's blood pressure and is now putting the equipment away.

MARY: I wish you would shut that racket up while I'm tryin' to finish up in here!

MOM: (*oblivious to Mary's comment*). What time is it Mary? Are you sure my son hasn't been here?

MARY: Now wouldn't he had stopped by here if he had? Why are you so uptight anyway?

MOM: (*smiling*). I'm hopin' for a big surprise today.

MARY: I knew somethin' was itchin' you. (*Sits down in chair by window*.) You have been hyper all mornin'! Playin' with those school children like you was ten years old! Causin' all that commotion in the lobby.

MOM: I was tryin' to relate to those youngins'. My grandchildren are comin' today and I wanted to figure out what's going to be on their minds.

MARY: I don't envision you havin' any problems relatin' to immature minds. Shouldn't be no problem at all.

MOM: No, but your mouth sure is a problem! I'll have you know I'm pretty smart when it comes to dealin' with children. I'd like to think I'm still a child...at heart anyway.

MARY: At brain you mean.

MOM: (*walking towards window*). I grew up in a family that let us be kids. Seems like kids today can't be kids no more. All that, pardon the expression, sex. Whenever Mikey tells me about somethin' on the news it's just filled with all types of violence... (*Gazing out window.*) I'll tell you what the problem is, Mary...

MARY: (*grabs a magazine and sits down*). What's that, hun? (*Flips through magazine.*)

MOM: The problem is there ain't no trees.

MARY: (*rises from chair, walks over to window and looks out*). Yup. No trees. That gets me horny!

MOM: I shouldn't think that I would have to explain such a thing to a woman of your experiences.

MARY: Explain. Explain.

MOM: Trees! Wilderness! You see, I grew up under the trees. I went crawdad fishin' with the boys. I saw nature first hand. I witnessed live births of everything from opossums to cows. Woo, Mary, have you ever seen a big fat cow havin' a baby?

MARY: (*walks over to medicine cart and begins organizing*). Yes, Ma'am. When I gave birth to my first child there was this mirror lookin' me straight in the eye! I said: Lord, I don't care who has seven years of bad luck, that mirror has got to go! I busted that sucker wide open!

MOM: Mary, you are not fat. I think you have a self-image

problem.

MARY: (*pulling Oreo from apron*). Self-image? I think you mean a self-*indulgence* problem. (*Takes bite of cookie.*) Self-image? Really! Honey, I was raised dirt poor and there wasn't no time to be dealin' with developin' a self-image. The only thing I was worried about developin' was my figure. (*Devours a whole cookie.*) Give me some food and watch it develop! (*Writing on clipboard.*) Self-image. Really!

MOM: I didn't know you grew up poor.

MARY: It wasn't all that bad. I guess it was sort of like livin' under your trees. I mean, I learned to take care of myself. What family I had allowed for a lot of love. My father wasn't too much on providin', but I always knew he loved us kids.

MOM: We never had too much on the materialistic side either. (*After a pause.*) Strugglin's part of realizin' what life is all about, I reckon. Course, I don't need to be tellin' you that. (*Mary sits down on the edge of the bed.*) Heck, it's a struggle for you to just make the bed.

MARY: You better jump back! I've been emptyin' bed pans for the likes of you for twenty some years now and I'll be dogged if I'll sit here and listen to yo' back talk!

MOM: Mary, I sure have enjoyed your company over the past few years.

MARY: (*taken aback.*) Say what?

33

MOM: You are the only one around here that treats us like part of the livin'.

MARY: If you like livin' so much, then why are you rushin' yo death?

MOM: I'm not rushin' my death. I just want my son to think I am dyin' so he'll bring my grandchildren to see me.

MARY: (rises, walks to dresser). Oh, yeah, I remember you tellin' me about that family. I always heard white folks lived peculiar, but I still can't figure your son out. (*Takes a peek in drawer, looking for cookies.*)

MOM: I figure if Kate thinks I'm gonna die in the next few months she won't mind sendin' the kids over to see me...no matter what her problem is with me.

MARY: Her problem? She is the problem! Honey, If I was you, the first time she pulled somethin' on me I would have slapped the taste right outta her mouth!

MOM: No such doin'.

MARY: Force is a powerful tool when used correctly. How come you never used any? I don't mean physical force, I mean goin' and gettin' a lawyer or somethin'.

MOM: I never wanted to come between my son and his wife. (*After a pause.*) Besides...I knew I would see my grandbabies someday.

MARY: (*crosses to door, accidentally drops clipboard*). Well, you do things your way and I'll do things my way—a good swift kick in the ... (*Just as she bends down to pick up clipboard the door swings open and hits her on the backside.*)

(*Mike enters.*)

MIKE: Oh, excuse me, I should have knocked first.

MARY: That's okay. That's what God gave me all this paddin' for. (*Crosses to medicine cart*).

(*Mary exits with cart.*)

MOM: (*raising her voice to be heard*). Self-image, Mary! Self-image!

MIKE: How are you feeling? (*He places flowers on the dresser and puts a brown paper bag in the top dresser drawer.*)

MOM: (*laying it on thick*). The misery. Oh, sometimes I just don't know how I can make it through another day. I've been laid up in this chair... (*Slowly eases into chair.*) all afternoon.

MIKE: The nurse told me the doctor was out of town today. I guess I will have to talk to him tomorrow.

MOM: (*to herself*). Wasn't that convenient.

MIKE: What was that?

MOM: He must be at the convent.

MIKE: Convent?

MOM: Yes, he likes to go there to see the ladies...I mean his sister. His sister is a nun ya know. Or perhaps you didn't. I can't say as he is too religious, but boy his sister sure is...Well, you know how those nuns are. (*Wipes her perspiring forehead with a tissue.*)

MIKE: I've heard.

MOM: So how are you feelin'?

MIKE: I'm fine. (*Searching for the right thing to say.*) It sure was a nice day today, wasn't it?

MOM: I wouldn't know. The curtains have been closed.

MIKE: (*opening curtains*). Seventy-five degrees.

MOM: Really?

MIKE: Picked those flowers myself.

MOM: They're beautiful.

MIKE: I'm glad you think so.

MOM: My favorites.

MIKE: I know.

MOM: Nice of you to remember.

MIKE: (*after an awkward pause*). I don't know what to say.

MOM: About what?

MIKE: About Kate and the kids.

MOM: What about them?

MIKE: (*sitting down.*) Do you remember me telling you about Kate's visits to the clinic?

MOM: Vaguely.

MIKE: It seems as though Kate has been seeing a psychiatrist of some sort. His name is Dr. Bigelow. Bigelow! What a name. Well, I called Dr. Bigelow's office on a hunch that Kate's problems might have something to do with the kids or possibly you. (*Sighs.*) Life is really meant for something else. I mean humans shouldn't be allowed such a divine occurrence as life...

36

MOM: What kind of thinking is that? Your father used to love to ponder things like that...

MIKE: (*interrupting*). Please let me get this over with. I feel so helpless. (*Pauses.*) Dr. Bigelow wouldn't tell me much. I had to pretend I already knew what was wrong with Kate as it was. The doctor said Kate identifies you with her own grandmother...

MOM: Isn't that a good thing?

MIKE: I wish. I dug deeper and called some of her relatives. As it turns out her grandmother was mentally ill and had to be committed to some sort of state institution. Kate's father felt a strong tie to his mother and insisted that the entire family visit her in the institution on a regular basis. (*Mike sits next to Mom.*) Kate hated those visits. While Kate was still relatively young there was a fatal accident involving her grandmother. I don't know where Kate's parents were at the time, but it seems as though her grandmother accidentally killed Kate's younger brother. Although it was reported as an accident no one really knew what actually took place, except for Kate. But she was never able to talk about it in any meaningful way. (*Realizing the conversation is not headed in a good direction, Mom looks away from Mike.*)   The family was in shock and eventually torn apart by the tragedy. That's probably why I never heard any details before. Kate was affected worse than anyone obviously.

MOM: (*slowly stands and crosses to bed away from Mike*). Let's not talk about such things today, Michael. It was such a lovely day. The sunshine was tryin' so hard to peek through the curtains this mornin'. (*Excited, almost childlike*). Oh, and Mary and I had such a wonderful chat. Have you ever met Mary? Mary is just a wonder. She's a nurse, you know. Well, of course you have met Mary…Yes, Mary is just a wonder.

MIKE: (*rising form chair*). You're not making this any easier.

MOM: (*turns towards him, quickly, harshly*). Am I supposed to? (*Beat.*) I'm sorry. I didn't mean to snap at you. I love you Michael. Do you know that? (*Trying not to cry.*) You were always my favorite son.

MIKE: (*moving towards her*). I was your only son, Mom.

MOM: (*takes his arm for support*). That doesn't matter. I know you would have been my favorite no matter how many sons I might have had. You were such a sweet little boy. (*She releases his arm and walks to dresser. She takes picture and walks towards window.*) I love you so much.

MIKE: (*watching her closely*). I love you too.

MOM: I don't see any way out of this so why don't you just say it and get it over with.

MIKE: It's not the easiest thing I have ever had to tell you, mother. It's not just something I can...

MOM: You're right. I do apologize (*Retrieves cane next to chair.*) Words were always hard for you. I blame that on your father. You came by it honestly. He never encouraged you much. Course he didn't really know how. He wanted to let you kids grow up to be individuals, but he contradicted himself with all those rules he expected us to follow. Every time you came home with a foreign thought, he would shoot ya down.

MIKE: It wasn't so bad.

MOM: He tried though, tried real hard. (*Mom fights back tears.*)

MIKE: Sometimes trying is pretty nice.

MOM: (*places picture in top dresser drawer*). Son, could you please come back another day? I'm not feelin' too well right now. I think I need a little time alone.

MIKE: (*crosses to Mom, kisses her forehead*). Mom, there is something else I need to tell you.

MOM: I can't hear anything right now let alone comprehend it. Please wait and tell me later.

MIKE: But I think you can handle this...

MOM: (*sharply*). Please leave! I just need some time to be alone. You understand, don't you? (*She turns her back to him.*)

MIKE: (*surprised at her resolve, but also understanding, he crosses to door*). Of course. (*After a pause and no*

39

response from Mom, he opens the door.) I'll see you soon, I love you.

(*Mike exits*.)

CURTAIN

END OF SCENE TWO

SCENE THREE

Several days later, Mom's bedroom.

Lights rise. The room is very somber. Mom is sitting up in bed. Mary is fluffing the pillows behind her back.

MARY: Why didn't you tell me you was tellin' the truth?

MOM: Truth about what?

MARY: Don't pull that jive honkey stuff on me. I can't believe that doctor didn't report this to us. I'll never know how you got him to keep his mouth shut.

MOM: The head nurse knows. I forced, you know—a swift kick...for him and her not to tell anybody else.

MARY: Why in heavens not?

MOM: It's just what I said about bein' treated as part of the livin'. If everyone knew that I only had a few more months to live they would treat me worse than they already do.

MARY: You know better than that.

MOM: I've been here for a good spell now and all I have seen is old men wearin' diapers, eighty-year-old women goin' to hospitals to have limbs cut off their fragile old bodies because of diabetes and bed sores! This place has death written all over it. It's the longest funeral I have ever been to and I'll be durned if I'm gonna be treated like one of them. (*Points to door.*)

41

MARY: It's okay, honey. It's alright. (*Stroking Mom's head.*) You're gonna be alright.

MOM: (*starting to laugh*). It's already started. I wouldn't have expected you...

MARY: (*pulling her hand back*). Now wait a minute! If you think you are gonna get special treatment from ol' Mary, you had better think twice! (*Mary pulls a pillow out from under Mom*). You can fix your own pillows from now on, child! I ain't changin' any bed pans for ya neither. Dyin' or no dyin', you can make it to the toilet!

MOM: (*smiling*). Not even for a package of Oreos? Top drawer right side.

MARY: Who buys those things for you, anyway?

MOM: What do you think that brown paper bag that my son brings in every week has in it? He thinks I adore Oreos.

MARY: You ol' goat! (*They both laugh.*) Oh, I almost forgot to give you this. (*Pulls envelope from pocket.*)

MOM: What is it?

MARY: Your son gave it to me before he left. Said he would be back tonight, but he wanted you to have this before you went to sleep yesterday. That's just like me to forget.

MOM: I don't think I'm up to readin' it, would you mind?

MARY: Where are those Oreos? (*Mary crosses to dresser and gets cookies.*) Well, now of course I'll read this for you. (*Mary crosses to chair and sits. She gets a cookie, takes a bite, opens envelope and begins reading the letter aloud.*) "Mom, I told you that I would not break my promise and I haven't... (*Interrupting the letter.*) What promise?

MOM: Will you just read the letter. (*Mom rises out of bed, gets her cane, and walks to window. She sits down in chair, looks out as Mary continues reading.*)

MARY: Here goes, "Kate didn't want the kids to see you. I couldn't bring the kids over and introduce them to you because Kate would be sure to find out about it. I don't think that would be wise in her condition...

Lights begin to fade. Mike's voice can be heard overlapping Mary's. When lights are completely down, only Mike's voice can be heard. There is a faint warm glow seeping through the window, illuminating Mom's face—her every expression can be seen.

MIKE: I asked the kid's school if they could sponsor a field trip that would benefit both the school and the community. School kids will visit a convalescent center and learn while older people enjoy the company of the children. They loved my idea. I was able to help coordinate and the principal cut through all the usual red tape once he heard about you. Those kids you were playing with the other day are your very own grandchildren. Because they've changed so much from the baby pictures you have of them, I had Mary shuffle them your way. Please understand, I couldn't tell you at first because I didn't know how you would react or if my plan would even work. I didn't want to get your expectations too high. I had to keep it a secret for everyone's sake. Someday when Kate can deal with her problem, I will tell the kids about you. In the meantime, the school found the trip so educational that they plan to repeat it once a week as a special project. Now it's our secret! I love you, Mom. Your son, Mikey.

(*Lights fade.*)

CURTAIN

END

www.ingramcontent.com/pod-product-compliance
Lightning Source LLC
Chambersburg PA
CBHW020438030426
42337CB00014B/1309